S0-ABD-359

"ASPIRE TO INSPIRE"

From: **Joseph A. Hayberger**
amdream@bex.net

To Elena, who was born with the "Heart of a Teacher"...

YOUR GIFTS AND PASSION ARE

THE INSPIRATION FOR THIS BOOK!

And to all the teachers of CLS who exemplify

the beautiful qualities illustrated on these pages...

YOU HOLD A SPECIAL PLACE IN MY HEART!

HEART *of a* TEACHER
Copyright © 2009 by Simple Truths, LLC

Published by Simple Truths
1952 McDowell Road, Suite 300
Naperville, Illinois 60563
800-900-3427

All rights reserved. No portion of this book may be reproduced, stored in a retrieval system
or transmitted in any form by any means—except for brief quotations in printed reviews—
without the prior written permission of the publisher.

Simple Truths is a registered trademark.

Scriptures noted NIV are taken from the HOLY BIBLE: NEW INTERNATIONAL
VERSION®. Copyright © 1973, 1978, 1984 by International Bible Society. Used by
permission of Zondervan Publishing House. All rights reserved.
Scriptures noted LB are taken from The Living Bible, Copyright © 1971. Used by
permission of Tyndale House Publishers, Inc., Wheaton, Illinois 60189. All rights reserved.
Scriptures noted NCV are taken from the New Century Version. Copyright © 2005 by
Thomas Nelson, Inc. Used by permission. All rights reserved.
Scriptures noted CEV are taken from the Contemporary English Version. Copyright © 1995
by American Bible Society. Used by permission.
Scriptures noted KJV are taken from the King James Version of the Bible.

Design and production: Koechel Peterson & Associates, Inc., Minneapolis, MN

Printed in the United States of America

WOZ 10 9 8 7 6 5 4 3 2

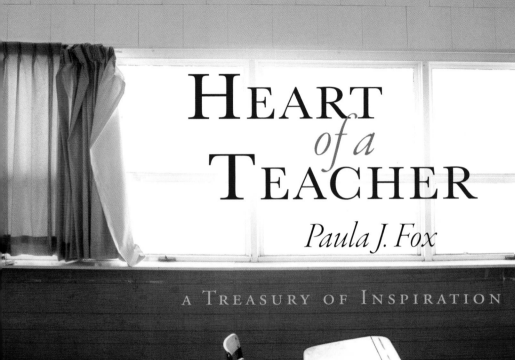

Heart
of a
Teacher

Paula J. Fox

A Treasury of Inspiration

FOREWORD

BY MAC ANDERSON | FOUNDER, SIMPLE TRUTHS

One of the things I love most about life is that when you wake up each morning, you never know if you might meet someone who will forever make a difference in your life.

It was about to happen on August 19, 2008. On that day, my assistant handed me a stack of mail, and sitting on top was a letter from Paula Fox, a Simple Truths customer. She said, "Mac, I love your books, and I also love to write poetry. So I wanted to share something I wrote called . . . *The Second Mile*.

Well, as you might imagine, we receive a lot of manuscripts, poems, quotes and ideas from our customers. Even though I'm grateful for all of them, most do not generate a "wow" response. This one did, however, and I picked up the phone to call Paula.

After a wonderful conversation and discovering that she had been a teacher for 30 years, I asked her if she could write a poem about teaching that we could use in a book we were considering. She said, "Sure, I'd love to!"

The rest, as they say, is history! A few weeks later she sent me her poem called "Heart of a Teacher." It was absolutely beautiful, and I immediately knew that Paula Fox was the writer whom I had been looking for to capture the essence of teaching.

On a personal note, however, one of the reasons I wanted to publish a book on teaching was to honor the teachers who had made a difference in my life. I grew up in Trenton, Tennessee, a small town of 5,000 people. I have wonderful memories of those first 18 years. And during those years, there were two teachers who I can say, with certainty, helped to make me who I am today.

The first was Ms. Bridges, who taught me in the 4th grade. She was amazing! I'll never forget her beautiful smile and her passion for teaching. She made learning so much fun and made all of us feel as though we could do anything we wanted to do. The positive seeds she planted in my head are still growing!

Then there was Fred Culp, my history teacher in high school. To this day, he is still the funniest person I've ever met. In addition to loving his history class, he taught me that a sense of humor, especially laughing at yourself, can be one of life's greatest blessings. He also, more than any teacher I ever had, made learning so much fun. His class was always the highlight of my day!

So, if you're a teacher, or if, like me, your life was greatly influenced by a teacher, you're going to love this book! The inspirational stories, the photographs, the quotes and Paula Fox's beautiful, original poems will find a special place in your heart.

Enjoy *Heart of a Teacher*.

Heart of a Teacher
by Paula J. Fox

THE CHILD ARRIVES like a mystery box . . .

with puzzle pieces inside

some of the pieces are broken or missing . . .

and others just seem to hide

HEART OF A

TEACHER

But the HEART of a teacher can sort them out . . .

and help the child to see

the potential for greatness he has within . . .

a picture of what he can be

Her goal isn't just to teach knowledge . . .

by filling the box with more parts

it's putting the pieces together . . .

to create a work of art

THE HEART

HEART OF A TEACHER

The process is painfully slow at times . . .

some need more help than others

each child is a work in progress . . .

with assorted shapes and colors

First she creates a classroom . . .

where the child can feel safe in school

where he never feels threatened or afraid to try . . .

and kindness is always the rule

She knows that a child

        can achieve much more

        when he feels secure inside

when he's valued and loved . . .

        and believes in himself . . .

        and he has a sense of pride

She models and teaches good character . . .

and respect for one another

how to focus on strengths . . . not weaknesses . . .

and how to encourage each other

She gives the child the freedom he needs . . .

to make choices on his own

so he learns to become more responsible . . .

and is able to stand alone

He's taught to be strong and think for himself

as his soul and spirit heal

and the puzzle that's taking shape inside . . .

has a much more positive feel

The child discovers the joy that comes

from learning something new...

and his vision grows as he begins

to see all the things he can do

A picture is formed as more pieces fit . . .

an image of the child within

with greater strength and confidence . . .

and a belief that he can win!

All because a hero was there . . .

in the HEART of a teacher who cared

enabling the child to become much more . . .

than he ever imagined . . . or dared

A teacher with a HEART for her children . . .

knows what teaching is all about

she may not have all the answers . . .

but on this . . . she has no doubt

When asked which subjects she loved to teach,

she answered this way and smiled . . .

"It's not the subjects that matter . . .

It's all about teaching the CHILD"

FIRST DAYS

by Elena C. Fox

THINK BACK TO SOME of your most memorable "first days." We have so many first days in our lives that it would be impossible not to remember at least one . . . your first day of school, your first day in a new place or on a new team, your first day of marriage, first day at a new job, first day of being a parent, etc.

First days are milestones in our lives. They mark the beginning of a new experience or journey. They are also filled with mixed emotions. They can be a little frightening as we step into the unknown, but they can also inspire us as they give us fresh hope for the future.

The principle here is that first days are powerful, and we can use them as turning points in our lives. If we have made some mistakes, we can use our first days as new beginnings to leave the past behind and learn from it as we start over. If we have had success, we can build on it and make it stronger. First days give us an opportunity to grow and change and become a better person.

This principle applies to both the way we see ourselves and the way we view others. As we extend grace to others, we give them a "first day" chance to start over . . . to leave the past behind and create a new future. This principle applies to everyone, but it is especially true for teachers.

As teachers, we are guaranteed at least one "first day" a year—a new school year, a new class, a new experience teaching. And we also have an opportunity to give each student in our class a life-changing "first day" experience . . . a chance to make a fresh start . . . to leave past mistakes and failures behind and begin a new and better life in school.

I want to share a story that perfectly illustrates this point. It is a story about a little girl named Trisha. Trisha was born into a family of teachers who had taught her that reading was the key to knowledge. She watched her older brother as he read his schoolbooks and could hardly wait for the day when she would learn to read.

This is part of a convocation speech that my daughter gave quite a few years back for her fellow students graduating with a degree in education. I love her passion as a teacher to give each child a fresh start in her classroom and a chance to become the best version of themselves.

But when Trisha finally started school, she found that she was not able to understand the words like the other boys and girls. No matter how hard she tried, the letters jumbled together, and she saw only confusion. Trisha fell further and further behind. The other children laughed and made fun of her, and she began to believe that she was not smart.

By the time Trisha entered fifth grade, she had lost all confidence in herself. That was the year she met Mr. Falker. He was different. He praised Trisha's talents, and he wouldn't tolerate the other children teasing her. Mr. Falker realized that Trisha didn't know how to read, but he knew that she could with some help.

He recruited a reading specialist, and together they worked with Trisha after school. They helped her to write the letters and hear the sounds until one day Mr. Falker handed her a book and she read it all by herself. She didn't even notice the tears in his eyes.

This is a true story. The little girl is Patricia Polacco, the famous children's author, and *Thank You, Mr. Falker* is the twenty-sixth book that she has written.

Mr. Falker gave her a fresh new start when she walked into his fifth grade class on that "first day" of school. He didn't judge her by what other teachers had said or written about her. And he made a difference in her life.

We can all make a difference in the world . . . one student at a time . . . by using "first days" with wisdom and grace, giving each individual the chance to start over and become the best that they can be.

The wisest and best teachers

TEACH FROM THE HEART,

not from the book.

AUTHOR UNKNOWN

IF A CHILD **CAN'T LEARN**
THE WAY WE TEACH,
maybe we should teach
the way they learn.

IGNACIO ESTRADA

"BEAUTIFUL CRAYONS"
by Paula J. Fox

I believe that
every child is
special and has
something of
value to
contribute to
our world.
I wrote this
poem as a
reminder that it
is our job as
teachers to help
everyone in
our class
to feel
"needed" and
"important"...
because
they are!!

Every year brings a new class of students . . .
    like crayons we find in school
    assorted sizes, shapes, and colors
    some are warm . . . some totally cool

Some are sharp . . . some very dull . . .
    some lost along the way
    Some have a bright and cheerful tone
    others more dark and grey

They all have names . . . some are common ones
    . . . easy to recognize
    Others are weird and hard to pronounce
    all special in God's eyes

Some of them . . . look fresh and new . . .
    while others appear well worn
    Some are shiny . . . some have sparkles
    many are broken and torn

But each one plays an important part . . .
    regardless of appearance
    as together they create a masterpiece
    with contrast, shadows, and brilliance

If we only used our favorite colors . . .
    and excluded all the rest
    our artwork would be boring
    and we'd miss out on God's best

It takes ALL the colors in the rainbow . . .
    with each varied tone and hue
    to give depth and meaning to our picture
    and enrich our point of view

It's the same with the children God created . . .
    each has something to give
    adding value and beauty in their own way
    to the world in which we live

The Story of Mark Eklund
(a true story)
by Sister Helen Mrosla

He was in the first third grade class I taught at Saint Mary's School in Morris, Minnesota. All thirty-four of my students were dear to me, but Mark Eklund was one in a million. Very neat in appearance, he had that happy-to-be-alive attitude that made even his occasional mischievousness delightful.

Mark talked incessantly. I had to remind him again and again that talking without permission was not acceptable. What impressed me so much, though, was his sincere response every time I had to correct him for misbehaving. "Thank you for correcting me, Sister!" I didn't know what to make of it at first, but before long I became accustomed to hearing it many times a day.

One morning my patience was growing thin when Mark talked once too often, and then I made a novice teacher's mistake. I looked at Mark and said, "If you say one more word, I am going to tape your mouth shut!" It wasn't ten seconds later when Chuck blurted out, "Mark is talking again." I hadn't asked any of the students to help me watch Mark, but since I had stated the punishment in front of the class, I had to act on it. I remember the scene as if it had occurred this morning. I walked to my desk, very deliberately opened my drawer, and took out a roll of masking tape. Without saying a word, I proceeded to Mark's desk, tore off two pieces of tape, and made a big X with them over his mouth. I then returned to the front of the room. As I glanced at Mark to see how he was doing, he winked at me. That did it! I started laughing. The class cheered as I walked back to Mark's desk, removed the tape, and shrugged my shoulders. His first words were, "Thank you for correcting me, Sister."

At the end of the year, I was asked to teach junior-high math. The years flew by, and before I knew it, Mark was in my classroom again. He was more handsome than ever and just as polite. Since he had to listen carefully to my instruction in the "new math," he did not talk as much in ninth grade as he had in third. One Friday, things just didn't feel right. We had worked hard on a new concept all week, and I sensed that the students were frowning, frustrated with themselves, and edgy with one another. I had to stop this crankiness before it got out of hand. So I asked them to list the names of the other students in the room on two sheets of paper, leaving a space

They may forget what you said . . . but they will never forget how you made them feel.

CARL W. BUECHNER

between each name. Then I told them to think of the nicest thing they could say about each of their classmates and write it down. It took the remainder of the class period to finish the assignment, and as the students left the room, each one handed me the papers. Charlie smiled. Mark said, "Thank you for teaching me, Sister. Have a good weekend." That Saturday, I wrote down the name of each student on a separate sheet of paper, and I listed what everyone else had said about that individual.

On Monday, I gave each student his or her list. Before long, the entire class was smiling. "Really?" I heard whispered. "I never knew that meant anything to anyone!" "I didn't know others liked me so much." No one ever mentioned those papers in class again. I never knew if they discussed them after class or with their parents, but it didn't matter. The exercise had accomplished its purpose. The students were happy with themselves and one another again.

That group of students moved on. Several years later, after I returned from vacation, my parents met me at the airport. As we were driving home, Mother asked me the usual questions about the trip, the weather, my experiences in general. There was a lull in the conversation. Mother gave Dad a sideways glance and simply said, "Dad?" My father cleared his throat, as he usually did before saying something important. "The Eklunds called last night," he began. "Really?" I said. "I haven't heard from them in years. I wonder how Mark is." Dad responded quietly. "Mark was killed in Vietnam," he said. "The funeral is tomorrow, and his parents would like it if you could attend." To this day, I can still point to the exact spot on I-494 where Dad told me about Mark.

I had never seen a serviceman in a military coffin before. Mark looked so handsome, so mature. All I could think at that moment was, "Mark, I would give all the masking tape in the world if only you would talk to me." The church was packed with Mark's friends. Chuck's sister sang "The Battle Hymn of the Republic." Why did it have to rain on the day of the funeral? It was difficult enough at the graveside. The pastor said the usual prayers, and the bugler played taps. One by one those who loved Mark took a last walk by the coffin and sprinkled it with holy water. I was the last one to bless the coffin. As I stood there, one of the soldiers who acted as pallbearer came up to me. "Were you Mark's math teacher?" he asked. I nodded as I continued to stare at the coffin. "Mark talked about you a lot," he said.

After the funeral, most of Mark's former classmates headed to Chuck's farmhouse for lunch. Mark's mother and father were there, obviously waiting for me. "We want to show you something," his father said, taking a wallet out of his pocket. "They found this on Mark when he was killed. We thought you might recognize it." Opening the billfold, he carefully removed two worn pieces of notebook paper that had obviously been taped, folded, and refolded many times. I knew without looking that the papers were the ones on which I had listed all the good things each of Mark's classmates had said about him. "Thank you so much for doing that," Mark's mother said. "As you can see, Mark treasured it." Mark's classmates started to gather around us. Charlie smiled rather sheepishly and said, "I still have my list. I keep it in the top drawer of my desk at home." Chuck's wife said, "Chuck asked me to put his in our wedding album." "I have mine too—in my diary," Marilyn said. Then Vicki, another classmate, reached into her pocketbook, took out her wallet, and showed her worn and frazzled list to the group. "I carry this with me at all times," Vicki said without batting an eyelash. "I think we all saved our lists." That's when I finally sat down and cried. I cried for Mark and for all his friends who would never see him again.

The density of people in society is so thick that we forget that life will end one day. And we don't know when that one day will be. So please, tell the people you love and care for that they are special and important. Tell them, before it is too late. ✤

Most of us end up with no more than
five or six people that remember us.
Teachers have thousands of people
who remember them for the rest of their lives.

ANDREW A. ROONEY

CREATIVE TEACHERS

DON'T JUST FOCUS ON THE DESTINATION . . .

they make the journey fun.

PAULA J. FOX

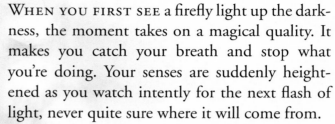

CATCHING FIREFLIES

BY PAULA J FOX

WHEN YOU FIRST SEE a firefly light up the darkness, the moment takes on a magical quality. It makes you catch your breath and stop what you're doing. Your senses are suddenly heightened as you watch intently for the next flash of light, never quite sure where it will come from.

Teaching children to "catch fireflies" can be a magical adventure as well. I'm not talking about the little lightning bugs found in nature, but the kind of "fireflies" that are those sparkling moments in our lives that brighten our day and make us feel better.

They are the small moments of brilliance and joy we discover in the course of a normal day that can bring light into our lives and make us want to share the good feelings. It may be an affirming word, an unexpected surprise, an act of kindness, a touch of beauty found in nature, a smile, a hug, and countless other examples of things that lift our spirits and make the world a better place.

"Fireflies" are "God moments". . . those times we suddenly become aware that God is in the moment, touching our lives in a special way, and we are encouraged and inspired by that personal touch.

Children catch on to this little treasure hunt quickly and delight in sharing what they find. One special first grade teacher decorates a large jar to put "fireflies" in. The children in her class use small pieces of yellow paper to write down or draw a picture of their "firefly." When they tell the class about it during the sharing time, they get to fold up their "firefly" and put it in the jar.

Not only is this little activity fun, but it teaches the children to look for the good things in their lives and to celebrate the small joys in each day, turning "firefly" moments into magical learning experiences.

In her book, *My Stroke of Insight,* Jill Bolte Taylor, Ph.D. tells us . . .

> *Our minds are highly sophisticated "seek and ye shall find" instruments. We are designed to focus on whatever we are looking for. If we seek red in the world then we will find it everywhere. Perhaps just a little in the beginning, but the longer we stay focused on looking for red, then before we know it, we will see red everywhere.*

If we focus on looking for "fireflies," we will see them everywhere!

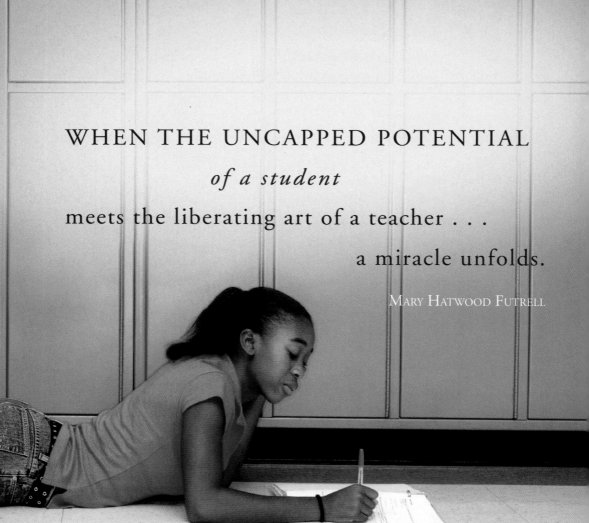

WHEN THE UNCAPPED POTENTIAL
of a student
meets the liberating art of a teacher . . .

a miracle unfolds.

MARY HATWOOD FUTRELL

52

THE WHISPER TEST
by Sally I. Kennedy

A young girl with a cleft palate and speech challenges was fortunate to be in a classroom setting with a wise teacher.

Each week the children would take the "whisper test." One at a time, the teacher called them forward. She would whisper in their ear a question, such as, "What did you have for breakfast this morning?" or "What is your mom's first name?" Then, when the child answered correctly, she'd exclaim, "Right! You pass!"

One week was a bit different. This time when the teacher called the little girl up, she whispered into her ear, "I wish you were my little girl."

That was a magical moment for the child. It was the turning point from her embarrassment and her insecurities. To know she was loved and valued changed her life.

To the loved,

a word of affection

is a morsel, but to

the love-starved,

a word of affection

can be a feast.

MAX LUCADO

Too often we underestimate
the power of a touch,
a smile, a kind word,
a listening ear, an honest compliment,
or the smallest act of caring,
all of which have the potential
to turn a life around.

LEO F. BUSCAGLIA

IF WE DO NOT INTENTIONALLY
ADD VALUE TO OTHERS,
WE PROBABLY UNINTENTIONALLY
SUBTRACT FROM THEM.

JOHN C. MAXWELL

A NEGATIVE OUTLOOK

is more of a handicap

than any physical injury.

CHRISTOPHER PAOLINI

"Exterminating . . . ANTS"

BY PAULA J. FOX

A teacher is an expert . . . at getting rid of ANTS
no exterminator can compete with her
The brains of little children . . . are sometimes filled with ANTS
and when they are . . . no learning can occur

It's a teacher's greatest enemy . . . and must be overcome
considering the problem that's at hand
One little ANT can grow into a mighty marching army
it will destroy if it's allowed to stand

We need to understand these ANTS in order to defeat them
they're not the tiny insects on the ground
These ANTS are far more powerful, destructive, and disarming
they attack a small child's mind and hold him down

They're *Automatic Negative Thoughts* . . . that fill the heart and soul
with feelings of discouragement and dread
And the only way to terminate this terrible assault
is with positive encouragement instead

PATS are most effective . . . in dealing with this pest
Positive Affirming Thoughts that heal
When used in massive quantities . . . they overcome the ANTS
resulting in more confidence that's real!

Children learn and grow . . . with a wise and caring teacher
. . . an expert in exterminating ANTS
By removing mental handicaps with lots of extra PATS
she helps each child to have a better chance!

TEACHERS LIVE IN THE MOMENT . . .

celebrating each success as it happens,

because every personal triumph

for a child, no matter how small,

inspires him to achieve more.

PAULA J. FOX

IF YOU MUST RAISE YOUR VOICE,
DO IT TO CHEER YOUR STUDENTS ON.

AUTHOR UNKNOWN

100 WAYS

to Encourage a Child

by Paula J. Fox

You did it!
Amazing! Hooray for you!
Such originality!
Extraordinary talent!
Sensational!
What creative ability!

Wow!
Fantastic!
That was great!
I'm proud of you!
Way to go!
Well done!
What an awesome victory!
You have what it takes!
Bravo!

Congratulations!
Super job!
Thumbs up!
You're number one!
Magnificent work!
Phenomenal!
I love what you have done!

What a clever idea!
You're a champion!
Stand up and take a bow!
Wonderful!
Fabulous!
Exceptional!
You're going places now!

You made it happen!
Incredible job!
All of your hard work shows!
Unbelievable effort!
Great attitude!
You are one of my heroes!

What beautiful work!
Nice going!
There's nothing that you can't do!
You've gone the extra mile!
You're the best!
I know I can count on you!

A brilliant performance!
Outstanding! Superb!
You're a bright and shining star!
Excellent job!
Spectacular!
You're on your way!
You'll go far!

I knew you could do it!
Keep up the good work!
You've made progress!
You are so smart!
What a trooper you are!
You should be proud!
You have a very brave heart!

You've discovered the secret!
You figured it out!
You're a winner!
Hip hip hooray!
You kept on trying!
You never gave up!
You're terrific!
You brighten my day!

I know you will make the right
choice! You can do it!
You're good at thinking things through!
You have earned my respect!
I trust your judgment!
I have confidence in you!

How thoughtful you are!
You inspired us all!
Thanks for helping!
You are so kind!
You make a great leader!
You're such an example!
What a sharp and sensitive mind!

Thank you for sharing with
others in class!
I like that you listen so well!
You're responsible!
You're so nice to your friends!
You are giving your best! I can tell!

I love your imagination!
You create such joy!
You're a gift!
You make life fun!
You make me laugh!
You give me such a lift!

You're a precious treasure!
You are one-of-a-kind!
No one else can take your place!
God created you for a purpose!
I love seeing your smiling face!

You touch my heart!
You're important to me!
I'm glad you're in my class too!
You're a special child!
You're a blessing!
I appreciate and celebrate You!

100 Way

o Encourage a Child

The Creation of a Teacher

AUTHOR UNKNOWN

The Good Lord was creating teachers. It was His sixth day of "overtime," and He knew that this was a tremendous responsibility, for teachers would touch the lives of so many impressionable young children. An angel appeared to Him and said, "You are taking a long time to figure this one out."

"Yes," said the Lord, "but have you read the specs on this order?"

TEACHER:
- must stand above all students, yet be on their level
- must be able to do 180 things not connected
  with the subject being taught
- must run on coffee and leftovers
- must communicate vital knowledge to all students daily
  and be right most of the time
- must have more time for others than for herself/himself
- must have a smile that can endure through pay cuts,
  problematic children, and worried parents
- must go on teaching when parents question every move
  and others are not supportive
- must have six pair of hands

"Six pair of hands," said the angel, "that's impossible."

"Well," said the Lord, "it is not the hands that are the problem. It is the three pairs of eyes that are presenting the most difficulty!"

The angel looked incredulous, "Three pairs of eyes . . . on a standard model?"

The Lord nodded His head. "One pair can see a student for what he is and not what others have labeled him as. Another pair of eyes is in the back of the teacher's head to see what should not be seen, but what must be known. The eyes in the front are only to look at the child as he/she 'acts out' in order to reflect, 'I understand and I still believe in you,' without so much as saying a word to the child."

"Lord," said the angel, "this is a very large project and I think you should work on it tomorrow."

"I can't," said the Lord, "for I have come very close to creating something much like Myself. I have one that comes to work when he/she is sick, teaches a class of children that do not want to learn, has a special place in his/her heart for children who are not his/her own, understands the struggles of those who have difficulty, and never takes the students for granted."

The angel looked closely at the model the Lord was creating and said, "It is too soft-hearted."

"Yes," said the Lord, "but also tough. You cannot imagine what this teacher can endure or do, if necessary."

"Can this teacher think?" asked the angel.

"Not only think," said the Lord, "but reason and compromise."

Those who can, do . . .
those who can do MORE,
teach.

AUTHOR UNKNOWN

The angel came closer to have a better look at the model and ran his finger over the teacher's cheek.

"Well, Lord," said the angel, "your job looks fine but there is a leak. I told you that you were putting too much into this model. You cannot imagine the stress that will be placed upon the teacher."

The Lord moved in closer and lifted the drop of moisture from the teacher's cheek. It shone and glistened in the light. "It is not a leak," He said. "It is a tear."

"A tear? What is that?" asked the angel. "What is a tear for?"

The Lord replied with great thought, "It is for the joy and pride of seeing a child accomplish even the smallest task. It is for the loneliness of children who have a hard time to fit in, and it is for compassion for the feelings of their parents. It comes from the pain of not being able to reach some children and the disappointment those children feel in themselves. It comes often when a teacher has been with a class for a year and must say good-bye to those students and get ready to welcome a new class."

"My," said the angel, "the tear thing is a great idea. You are a genius!"

The Lord looked somber. "I didn't put it there."

"Handle with Care"

by Paula J. Fox

A child's heart is fragile . . .
DON'T BREAK IT
A child's mind is open . . .
DON'T CLOSE IT
A child's soul is tender . . .
DON'T HARDEN IT
A child's spirit is joyful . . .
DON'T CRUSH IT

A GIFTED TEACHER

MAKES LEARNING A JOY

BY CAPTURING TEACHABLE MOMENTS

AND TURNING THEM INTO MAGICAL

LEARNING EXPERIENCES.

PAULA J. FOX

I LIKE NONSENSE,
IT WAKES UP THE BRAIN CELLS.
FANTASY IS A NECESSARY INGREDIENT IN LIVING.
IT'S A WAY OF LOOKING AT LIFE
THROUGH THE WRONG END OF A TELESCOPE,
WHICH IS WHAT I DO,
AND THAT ENABLES YOU
TO LAUGH AT LIFE'S REALITIES.

THEODORE "DR. SEUSS" GEISEL

"UPSIDE DOWN DAYS"
by Paula J. Fox

We call them "upside down days" . . . when things just fall apart
and nothing seems to go the way it's planned
Normal schedules get mixed up and kids seem to forget
the classroom rules they used to understand

That's when creative teachers will turn things "upside down"
making it a game for just one day
Completely changing everything . . . and the order things are done
doing routine tasks a different way

Just thinking of things "upside down" makes everything more fun
kids smile when they are more inclined to frown
Mistakes don't seem like problems then . . . they take things more in stride
They can laugh and work at turning things around

Sometimes the lessons taught in school aren't always found in books . . .
important things like . . . F L E X I B I L I T Y
And nothing helps to make the point like showing how it's done . . .
making "upside down days" . . . FUN! . . . like they should be!

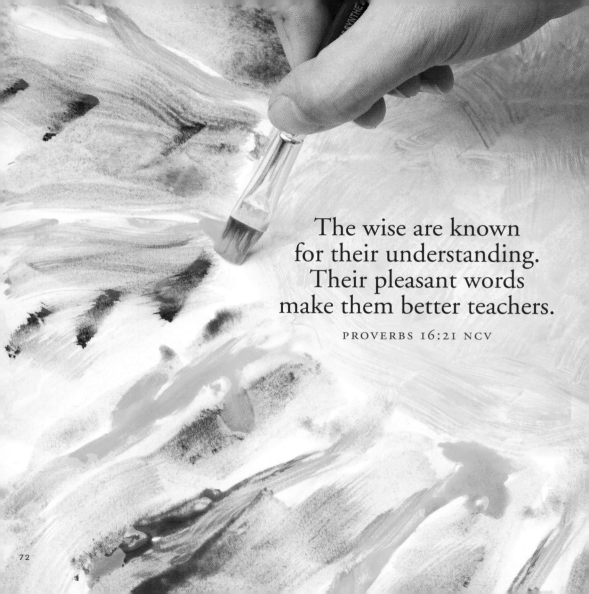

The wise are known
for their understanding.
Their pleasant words
make them better teachers.

PROVERBS 16:21 NCV

The Parable of the Child
by Steve Goodier

A YOUNG SCHOOLTEACHER had a dream that an angel appeared to him and said, "You will be given a child who will grow up to become a world leader. How will you prepare her so that she will realize her intelligence, grow in confidence, develop both her assertiveness and sensitivity, be open-minded, yet strong in character? In short, what kind of education will you provide that she can become one of the world's truly GREAT leaders?"

The young teacher awoke in a cold sweat. It had never occurred to him before—any ONE of his present or future students could be the person described in his dream. Was he preparing them to rise to ANY POSITION to which they may aspire? He thought, How might my teaching change if I KNEW that one of my students were this person? He gradually began to formulate a plan in his mind.

This student would need experience as well as instruction. She would need to know how to solve problems of various kinds. She would need to grow in character as well as knowledge. She would need self-assurance as well as the ability to listen well and work with others. She would need to understand and appreciate the past, yet feel optimistic about the future. She would need to know the value of lifelong learning in order to keep a curious and active mind. She would need to grow in understanding of others and become a student of the spirit. She would need to set high standards for herself and learn self-discipline, yet she would also need love and encouragement, that she might be filled with love and goodness.

His teaching changed. Every young person who walked through his classroom became, for him, a future world leader. He saw each one, not as they were, but as they could be. He expected the best from his students, yet tempered it with compassion. He taught each one as if the future of the world depended on his instruction.

After many years, a woman he knew rose to a position of world prominence. He realized that she must surely have been the girl described in his dream. Only she was not one of his students, but rather his daughter. For of all the various teachers in her life, her father was the best.

I've heard it said that "Children are living messages we send to a time and place we will never see." But this isn't simply a parable about an unnamed schoolteacher. It is a parable about you and me—whether or not we are parents or even teachers. And the story, OUR story, actually begins like this:

"You will be given a child who will grow up to become…" You finish the sentence. If not a world leader, then a superb father? An excellent teacher? A gifted healer? An innovative problem solver? An inspiring artist? A generous philanthropist?

Where and how you will encounter this child is a mystery. But believe that his or her future may depend upon influence only you can provide, and something remarkable will happen. For no child will ever be ordinary to you again. And you will never be the same.

Teachers inspire the smallest hearts to grow big enough to change the world.

PAULA J. FOX

. . . a little child shall lead them.

ISAIAH 11:6 KJV

"LESSON FROM A LITTLE CHILD"
by Paula J. Fox

A class of three and four year olds
not yet in kindergarten
but one of them taught me a lesson
that won't soon be forgotten

I was teaching them how to show love to each other
and what it means to be kind
a "hands-on craft" was part of the lesson
to impress it on each little mind

As they wiggled and bounced around in their seats
they weren't listening very well
I wondered if they even heard a word
of what I was trying to tell

For the craft, each child was to make a card
as a gift for someone they love
to surprise them with an act of kindness
in a way they'd never think of

I noticed one child who hurried the task
quickly scribbling to finish his card
he sometimes made such a mess of things
and teaching him could be hard

He knew how to push every boundary
and when things didn't go his way
he'd frequently have a meltdown
and ruin everybody's day

He finished his card before the rest
and shoved it into my hand
I figured he didn't have a clue
what I wanted him to understand

Not feeling very kind-hearted myself
I reminded him . . . once more
that giving it to someone he loved would be kind
and that's what it was for

With a twinkle in his eye, he smiled and said,
"I know! . . . I'm giving it to *You!*"
It took me a moment to comprehend
then I realized . . . that he knew!

He knew exactly what he was doing
he had understood every part
more than just following directions
he was giving me a gift from his heart!

My heart exploded with love for this child
and I felt a wave of shame
he knew more about kindness than I did
I had just been playing the game

It's so easy to judge by the outside behavior
whether rules are followed or broken
but the heart of the child is what matters
feelings and words unspoken

No wonder God loves little children so much
with their hearts so fresh and pure
they can teach us a thing or two about love
they know what it is, for sure!

A teacher with WISDOM and UNDERSTANDING

listens to the HEART

of a child . . .

not just the words spoken.

PAULA J. FOX

"Whose Child Is This?"

AUTHOR UNKNOWN

"Whose child is this?" I asked one day
Seeing a little one out at play
"Mine," said the parent with a tender smile
"Mine to keep a little while
To bathe his hands and comb his hair
To tell him what he is to wear
To prepare him that he may always be good
And each day do the things he should"

"Whose child is this?" I asked again
As the door opened and someone came in
"Mine," said the teacher with the same tender smile
"Mine, to keep just for a little while
To teach him how to be gentle and kind
To train and direct his dear little mind
To help him live by every rule
And get the best he can from school"

"Whose child is this?" I asked once more
Just as the little one entered the door
"Ours," said the parent and the teacher as they smiled
And each took the hand of the little child
"Ours to love and train together
Ours this blessed task forever."

"A PARENT'S NOTE TO A TEACHER"

I'm the voice of a grateful parent
whose child was in your class . . .
the one who needed help to find his way

You've been a special blessing
as you helped my child succeed
and I'm thankful for the part you had to play

You gave him so much more
than just the lessons in the books
you gave him wings . . . so he could learn to fly

You ignited a flame within his soul
a passion to learn and grow . . .
to never give up and always be willing to try

Your encouragement inspired him
and your kindness was so real
but the thing that thrills my heart the most is this . . .

By building his self-confidence
you changed his life this year
he believes in himself . . . and a brighter future is his!

IT'S UP TO ME . . .

I've come to the frightening conclusion that I am
the decisive element in the classroom. It's my daily mood that
makes the weather. As a teacher, I possess a tremendous power
to make a child's life miserable or joyous.
I can be a tool of torture or an instrument of inspiration.
I can humiliate or humor, hurt or heal. In all situations,
it is my response that decides whether a crisis will be escalated
or de-escalated and a child humanized or de-humanized.

HAIM GINOTT

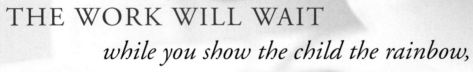

THE WORK WILL WAIT

while you show the child the rainbow,

BUT THE RAINBOW WON'T WAIT WHILE YOU DO THE WORK.

Patricia Clafford

RAINBOW MOMENT
by Paula J. Fox

There is something about a rainbow that is so breathtaking
it causes most people to stop what they are doing and look,
even if just for a moment.
And that moment we stop and look refreshes our soul.

Children love to stop and look at many things
that adults would just ignore and pass right on by.
But a rainbow moment . . . and the beauty and benefit
of living in that moment . . .
is fleeting and will soon be gone.

Children often learn best in those spontaneous moments
when they want to stop and look.
Their natural curiosity makes them want to stop
whatever they're doing and find out more
about something that interests them.
We call these "teachable moments" for obvious reasons.

The lesson in the rainbow is that
it's important to stop and look . . .
and teach the child what he's interested in experiencing
and learning at that moment,
because the teachable moment can't be recaptured later.

THE ANIMAL SCHOOL
by George H. Reavis

Once upon a time, the animals decided they must do something heroic to meet the problems of "a new world." So they organized a school.

They adopted an activity curriculum consisting of running, climbing, swimming and flying. To make it easier to administer the curriculum, all the animals took all the subjects.

The duck was excellent in swimming, in fact better than his instructor, but he made only passing grades in flying and was very poor in running. Since he was slow in running, he had to stay after school and also drop swimming in order to practice running. This was kept up until his webbed feet were badly worn and he was only average in swimming. But average was acceptable in school, so nobody worried about that except the duck.

The rabbit started at the top of the class in running, but had a nervous breakdown because of so much make-up work in swimming.

The squirrel was excellent in climbing until he developed frustration in the flying class, where his teacher made him start from the ground up instead of from the treetop down. He also developed a "charley horse" from overexertion and then got a "C" in climbing and a "D" in running.

The eagle was a problem child and was disciplined severely. In the climbing class he beat all the others to the top of the tree, but insisted on using his own way to get there.

At the end of the year, an abnormal eel that could swim exceedingly well, and also run, climb, and fly a little, had the highest average and was valedictorian.

The prairie dogs stayed out of school and fought the tax levy because the administration would not add digging and burrowing to the curriculum. They apprenticed their children to a badger and later joined the groundhogs and gophers to start a successful private school.

This story is one of my favorites for teachers. It makes such a great point about the importance of teaching to each child's strengths and not killing the "passion" within.
Paula J. Fox

"ALTHOUGH IT IS THE SMALLEST

OF ALL SEEDS,

IT GROWS LARGER

THAN ANY GARDEN PLANT

AND BECOMES A TREE."

MATTHEW 13:32 NIV

"Finding a Child's Passion"
by Paula J. Fox

God plants a seed of passion . . . in the heart of every child
like a special treasure buried underground
And like every seed that's planted . . . it takes a lot of care
to take root and grow . . . so the passion can be found

The challenge for a teacher . . . is to help each child to find
just what it is they really love to do
Without the proper nurturing . . . the seed within may die
and with it . . . any hope for greatness too

God created every child . . . with a purpose to fulfill
and equipped him with the talents to achieve
But in order to accomplish . . . all the great things he can do
he must follow his own passion . . . and believe

It takes a very wise . . . and dedicated teacher
to guide each child to this discovery
By encouraging the child . . . in the way that he is "bent"
he'll become the very best that he can be

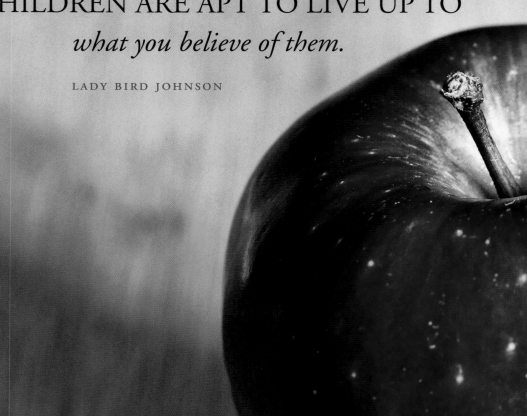

CHILDREN ARE APT TO LIVE UP TO

what you believe of them.

LADY BIRD JOHNSON

95

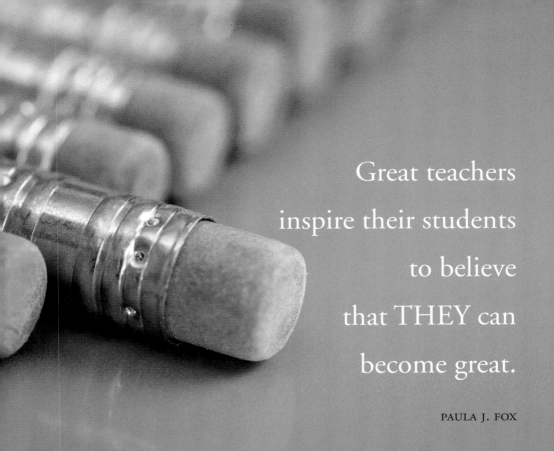

Great teachers
inspire their students
to believe
that THEY can
become great.

PAULA J. FOX

"A LOVING TEACHER"
by Pat McClain

Things our grown-up mind defies
Appear as giants in children's eyes.
A gentle touch upon her head
A simple word when kindly said.

Complete attention when she calls
Her knowing you have given all.
Correcting in a loving way.
Instilling trust in what you say.

Making her believe unique
The tiny flaw upon her cheek.
Admiring old and faded dresses.
Reminding her we all make messes.

Words of comfort you've softly spoken
A promise you've made
she knows won't be broken.
Your knowing her doll that was lost today
Is just as important as bills you can't pay.

Helping make her plans and schemes
Giving her hope and building her dreams.
All of this and so much more
Is in her mind forever stored.

They who touch her life awhile
Can either make or break that child.
Education is important, true,
But so much more, her faith in you.

You've weathered through the storm and strife;
You helped to build a small girl's life.
You're truly one to be admired.
For you gave more than was required.

ONE SPECIAL TEACHER

CAN MAKE

A POSITIVE DIFFERENCE

IN A CHILD'S ENTIRE LIFE

IN JUST ONE YEAR!

PAULA J. FOX

Here's to the kids

Here's to the kids who are different,
Kids who don't always get A's,
Kids who have ears
Twice the size of their peers,
And noses that go on for days

Here's to the kids who are different,
Kids they call crazy or dumb,
Kids who don't fit,
With the guts and the grit
To dance to a different drum

Here's to the kids who are different,
Kids with a mischievous streak,
For when they have grown,
As history has shown,
It's their difference that makes them unique

HERE'S TO THE KIDS WHO ARE DIFFERENT ©1982, DIGBY WOLF, UNW

Teachers Who Make a Difference

THIS POEM WAS FRAMED and hung in her office, and it defined her feelings about the children and teens who came to her for help with study skills and other school-related issues. She was their advocate and champion, always on their side . . . an education specialist, a teacher and counselor extraordinaire, and a hero in every sense of the word.

She "rescued" the many students who walked through her door with her wisdom, humor, and great compassion. I know from personal experience because she not only rescued a child I loved, but she helped him to discover his own giftedness and brilliance . . . and to believe in himself. She gave him the tools he needed to not only achieve in school, but to excel and be the great success in life he is today.

Her name was Dr. Clare B. Jones, Ph.D., and she died of cancer a few years back. I still grieve the loss of this wonderful teacher with a huge heart for the "kids who are different."

Here's to all the teachers who are like her . . . teachers who MAKE a difference!

IF KIDS COME TO US (EDUCATORS/TEACHERS)

FROM STRONG,

HEALTHY FUNCTIONING FAMILIES,

it makes our job easier.

IF THEY DO NOT COME TO US

FROM STRONG,

HEALTHY FUNCTIONING FAMILIES,

it makes our job more important.

BARBARA COLOR

Wedding Surprise

BY PAMELA ELLIOTT

THIS PAST SCHOOL YEAR I WAS PLEASED WHEN A STUDENT I HAD IN THIRD GRADE CAME BACK TO PERSONALLY INVITE ME TO HIS WEDDING. HE SAID I WAS THE ONLY TEACHER THAT HAD BELIEVED IN HIM. IT MADE ME FEEL SO WONDERFUL THAT HE WOULD REMEMBER ME AND THINK ENOUGH OF ME TO SHARE THE MOST IMPORTANT DAY OF HIS LIFE. I CAN'T TELL YOU HOW GREAT THAT MADE ME FEEL. IT MADE NOT ONLY MY DAY BUT ALSO THE REST OF MY SCHOOL YEAR.

Then the day of the wedding arrived. I sat on the aisle seat so I could at least see the groom. When he came down the aisle with his new bride, we exchanged smiles and it made me feel special. I went through the receiving line and got big hugs from his sister, then from him, and next his father and his mother. His mother was crying, don't all mothers cry at weddings?! I told her how pleased I was to share this special day and she said, "You've done so much for our son." I answered by saying that I was glad if I had, even though I wasn't sure what. His mother then said that she'd like to tell me what sometime, and I responded that I'd like that and sat back down. Soon after the head table was seated I felt a tug on my arm and it was the groom's father. He said, "You're wanted down front." I couldn't imagine why. As we approached his table he told me the groom wanted me to sit with his parents. I couldn't believe that on "his" special day he would even be thinking about me, let alone want me to sit with his parents. Then the groom got up and came down to my table and presented me with roses.

I was in such disbelief! I think I said something like, "This is your day, what are you doing?" He just grinned and went back to sit with his bride.

Then his parents said they wanted me to know "what" I had done for their son. They said that after he was in my class he had a really bad year where a teacher constantly put him down. He began writing that he was stupid, he was dumb, and that he hated himself. Then one day he went out into their barn with the intention of hanging himself. He thought of me and my faith in him and couldn't do it. His parents then thanked me for their son.

Needless to say I was overwhelmed with emotions. After I left the wedding reception, I cried all the way home. I have always promised myself that I would retire when I no longer enjoyed getting out of bed and heading for school. On that trip home I made a silent promise to this young man that as soon as I couldn't support my students I would quit.

That didn't seem enough somehow and a friend suggested I write this down and share it somewhere in order to affect a lot of teachers. Letting teachers know that they DO make a difference was a way for both the groom and me to really use this to help make a difference in someone else's life.

Someone suggested using the word inspire and I initially thought that was a good idea. But, after thinking awhile, the word inspire means to me to move toward something and I think this whole incident SHOUTS that we ALREADY make a difference whether we ever know it or not.

So keep up the good work and have a great year. This message comes from the groom and myself.

LET NO ONE EVER COME TO YOU
WITHOUT LEAVING BETTER AND HAPPIER.

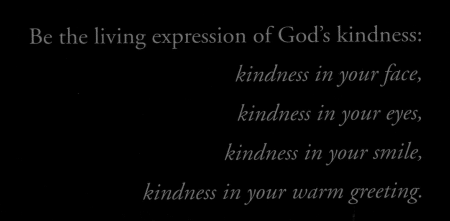

Be the living expression of God's kindness:

kindness in your face,

kindness in your eyes,

kindness in your smile,

kindness in your warm greeting.

MOTHER TERESA

"BODY LANGUAGE"

by Paula J. Fox

As I dropped him off in front of the school,
I watched him walk away
His body language said it all . . .
and it broke my heart that day

Just a little boy, only nine years old . . .
but he already felt defeat
You could see it . . . as he hung his head
and slowly shuffled his feet

His heart and soul had been damaged last year. . .
by a teacher who wasn't wise
She made him feel like a failure . . .
not worth much in her eyes

And of course, he believed it was all his fault . . .
as children usually do
It's hard for a child to achieve very much
when he thinks those things are true

But I prayed this year would be different . . .
that his teacher would be caring and kind
able to repair his broken spirit
and renew his tender mind

Mrs. Day was her name . . . my answer to prayer . . .
with a heart as big as they come
Adding value to each of her children
she encouraged every one

She touched the hearts of her students . . .
giving strength to conquer each fear
and all the kids in her fourth grade class
had their most successful year

They all believed they were winners . . .
including my little boy
when I picked him up toward the end of school
I noticed he walked out with JOY!

His body language was different this time . . .
he walked with his head held high
there was even a little bounce in his step . . .
He was ready now to fly!!!

NEVER LET A SINGLE DAY PASS
WITHOUT SAYING AN ENCOURAGING
WORD TO EACH CHILD.

*More people fail for lack of encouragment,
than for any other reason.*

Ruth Bell Graham

A TEACHER'S DASH

BY LINDA ELLIS

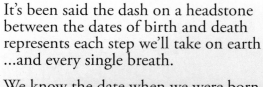

It's been said the dash on a headstone
between the dates of birth and death
represents each step we'll take on earth
...and every single breath.

We know the date when we were born,
but the following date can't be foreseen
and all the days that we will live
are in that little dash in between.

Though we all may strive to prosper
during our time here on earth,
it isn't the money in our bank account
that measures what our dash is worth.

Some deem themselves "successful"
if they can spend in large amounts,
but how you spend your only dash
is all that really counts.

When young minds want to understand
what is just beyond their reach,
a special soul is called upon
to enlighten ... and to teach.

A teacher chooses her career
not for prestige, wealth, or cash,
but because her heart is telling her
this is how to live her dash.

For he receives true satisfaction
from guiding and from giving;
fulfillment found in making a life ...
and not just making a living.

A good teacher has a tendency
to do more than what's required
to prepare and send into the world
each "dash" that she's inspired.

Teachers make a difference
in each young mind they embrace;
they mold our future in their classrooms
and make the world a better place.

© 2007 Linda Ellis, author of *The Dash*
www.lindaellis.net

CHILDREN ARE THE LIVING MESSAGES

WE SEND TO A TIME AND PLACE

WE MAY NEVER KNOW OR SEE.

AUTHOR UNKNOWN

"THE GIFT OF A TEACHER'S HEART"

by Paula J. Fox

When God was designing talents and gifts . . .
    He carefully crafted each one
but the Heart that He made for the Gift of Teaching . . .
    was beyond comparison!

He saved this important gift for last . . .
    spending time on every feature
creating His very best design
    for the special **Heart of a Teacher**

It's a **Heart of Humility** focused on others . . .
    unselfish in all its ways
with a spirit of love and gratitude
    never seeking to receive the praise

It's a **Heart of Generosity** . . .
    that gives more than the job will pay
It's not about money . . .
    but touching lives that may change the world someday

It's a **Heart of Joy** that makes learning fun . . .
    and finds delight in teaching
creating and capturing teachable moments
    for exploring . . . learning . . . reaching

It's a **Heart of Wisdom** that teaches truth . . .
    and accountability too
building character and integrity
    so each child will know what to do

It's a **Heart of Kindness** that's sensitive . . .
    to the feelings of a child
adding value and building self-confidence
    with encouraging words and a smile

It's a **Heart of Compassion** that reaches out . . .
    to the child with special needs
helping to overcome challenges
    making sure that he succeeds

It's a **Heart of Discernment** that understands . . .
    and has the insight to see
beyond what a child is like today
    to his potential . . . and what he can be

Teachers may not
        make a lot of money . . .
but they make a lot of difference.

PAULA J. FOX

It's a **Heart of Purpose** that knows what matters . . .
  is the treasure inside every heart
helping each child to find his own way
  to play a significant part

It's a **Heart of Passion** that inspires greatness . . .
  by lighting a fire within
empowering a child with the inner strength
  to go further than he's ever been

It's a **Heart of Patience** that never gives up . . .
  when the process seems much too slow
always searching for better solutions
  to help a child learn and grow

It's not easy being a Teacher . . .
  and this Heart takes a beating each day
sometimes it breaks for a hurting child
  and a piece is given away

But there's strength in the **Heart of a Teacher** . . .
  and a special vision to see
the difference you make in the heart of a child
  . . . can affect eternity!

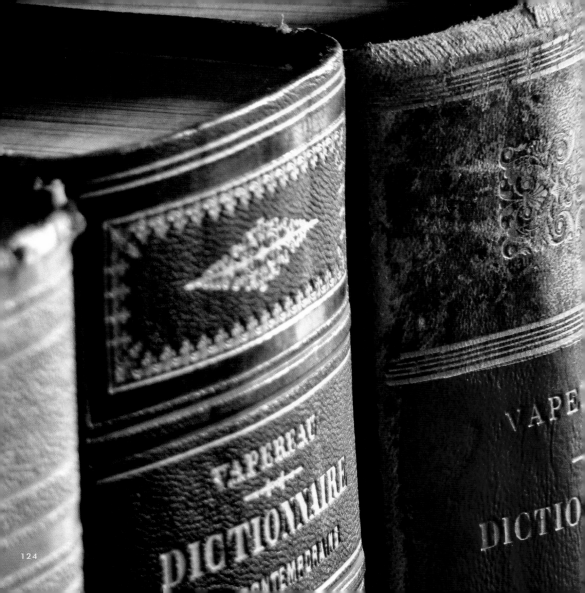

A HUNDRED YEARS FROM NOW,

it will not matter what my bank account was,

the sort of house I lived in, or the kind of car I drove.

But the world may be different

because I was important in the life of a child.

FOREST E. WITCRAFT

Paula J. Fox describes herself as a lifetime student whose passion is to continue learning and applying godly wisdom in her life so that she can share it with others. Her desire is to inspire and motivate others to live a life of purpose and significance. She is a teacher at heart with a degree in special education and 35 years experience teaching and leading all ages from preschool through adult.

She and her husband, Larry, have three grown children and she is now able to devote more of her time to writing. Besides being a teacher and leader in her own church, she is the founder and leader of L'dor (Ladies' day of renewal), a home-based Bible study for women. This ministry, which began over 25 years ago, meets weekly in homes where they worship together through songs and scriptures, sharing and studying God's Word together. Paula loves researching and writing her own lessons for L'dor as well as writing poetry and prose. She also enjoys speaking to women's groups and retreats.

Contact Paula Fox at paulajfox@live.com

If you have enjoyed this book we invite you to check out our entire collection of gift books, with free inspirational movies, at www.simpletruths.com. You'll discover it's a great way to inspire friends and family, or to thank your best customers and employees.

The
simple truths®
DIFFERENCE

For more information, please visit us at:
www.simpletruths.com
Or call us toll free... **800-900-3427**